T0245909

THE **GRADUATE SURVIVAL** GUIDE

5 MISTAKES

YOU CAN'T AFFORD TO MAKE

IN COLLEGE

"Refuse good advice and watch your plans fail;
take good counsel and watch them succeed."

Proverbs 15:22 (The Message)

THE GRADUATE SURVIVAL GUIDE

5 MISTAKES
YOU CAN'T AFFORD TO MAKE
IN COLLEGE

JADE WARSHAW

RAMSEY
PRESS

Published by Ramsey Press, The Lampo Group, LLC

Franklin, TN 37064

Content Development: Rick Prall and Erica Nebiker

Editors: Jessica Sly and Jordan Russ

Cover Design: Tim Newton, Chris Carrico, Chris Sandlin, and Heather Eikel

Interior Design: Tim Newton, Chris Carrico, Chris Sandlin, and Heather Eikel

ISBN: 979-8-8878-2044-6

Printed in the United States of America

24 25 26 27 28 JST 12 11 10 9 8

CONTENTS

Jade Warshaw... vi

Foreword by Dave Ramsey.. x

Mistake 01 // Student Loan Debt............................... 1

Mistake 02 // Credit Cards... 25

Mistake 03 // Dumb Choices...................................... 45

Mistake 04 // No Plan.. 65

Mistake 05 // No Money... 85

Resources.. 105

JADE WARSHAW

Hey there! I'm Jade. From here on out, just think of me as your protective older—yet surprisingly young-looking—sister. I'm so proud of you! You've come so far and accomplished so much. **Now you're ready to embark on yet another amazing adventure: college.**

I'm here to look out for you. Since I've had the chance to make all the mistakes in this book—and learn from them—**I want to share what works and what doesn't**. You are officially "my people," and I don't like anyone messing with my people— especially when it comes to something as important as your education and your money.

Give me a little bit of your time, and I'll be honest with you about the five mistakes you can't afford to make in college.

And trust me, I know firsthand about all five of these mistakes because I've made every single one of them. In fact, if there was a trophy for Mistake Champion, I'd have it displayed on my shelf. I learned all these lessons the hard way, which means you won't have to.

Here's something else that's helpful to know about my background: I got married one week after college graduation. Can you imagine that? And just a few months into our new married life, with college degrees in hand, my college sweetheart and **I realized that we were deeply in debt**. Here's how the major debts broke down:

> **$280,000 in student loans** (ouch!)
> **$20,000 in credit cards**
> **$50,000 in car loans** (yep, we each had one)
> **$100,000 on a town home**

The grand total was $460,052, to be exact. And it was absolutely, positively overwhelming. It was spirit-crushing! And it was all because, coming out of high school, we didn't have the blueprint. You know, the plan for how to handle all the finances related to college.

No one told us the best way to navigate our college years from a money standpoint. As a result, my husband and I both made the same financial slipups, sending us into almost half a million dollars of debt. (Yes, really!)

We spent the next seven and a half years after graduation working and sacrificing like crazy to clean up our debt and right our financial wrongs. **That time of life was very, very hard.** It was also very, very exhausting. I don't want that for you. Here are some of the things I *do* want for you:

- **I want you to have a solid plan as you navigate your college finances.**
- **I want you to graduate college with no student loan debt—and with money saved in the bank.**
- **I want you to be able to transition seamlessly into a job because you love it—not because you need a paycheck to pay off your student loans.**
- **I want you to come out of college with peace and freedom, ready to smash this life.**

It's my great honor—and great excitement—to help you do just that. Why? **Because getting control of your money—now—is a way to love yourself, your family, and your future well.**

- Jade

FOREWORD

DAVE RAMSEY

"Dave! Why in the world don't they teach this stuff in college?"

I had just finished teaching one of my first financial seminars when a lady walked up and hit me with that question. Over the next couple of years, more and more people asked me that same question after live events, at book signings, and on my call-in radio show.

It's no wonder why people ask about that. I've heard from millions of people who have completely wrecked their lives by boneheaded money mistakes that started in their college years. I'm a huge fan of education, but I don't think most colleges are really teaching kids what they need to know when it comes to handling money wisely.

I remember my broke finance professor telling me that successful businesses take advantage of sophisticated tools like "other people's money" and "good debt" to really win in the marketplace. I tried that advice when I graduated college—and it led straight to bankruptcy. I was more than $3 million in debt in my twenties!

It took me a long time to clean up that mess and learn how to handle money. I've spent the last few decades helping other people do that through *Financial Peace University (FPU)*. Now, every day on my radio show, I take calls from people all over the country who have really screwed up their lives because they started depending on debt. And a lot of it is student loan debt and credit card debt that can be traced back to lousy financial decisions they made in college.

Don't let that be you! There are some simple things that—if you learn them early enough, before you get into financial trouble—can completely change the direction of your life. You just need someone to show you how it works.

I've heard from millions of people who have completely wrecked their lives by boneheaded money mistakes that started in their college years.

That's where Jade Warshaw comes in. You'll get to know Jade and her story pretty well in *The Graduate Survival Guide*, but I want you to know two things about her before you even get started: Jade really hates debt, and Jade really loves students and helping them avoid making huge financial mistakes.

Why? Because Jade and her husband found themselves, as newlyweds after college graduation, in almost half a million dollars of debt. That included student loans, credit cards, and car loans—all the "normal" debt that gets so many people in trouble. Jade and Sam were normal by the world's standards and bought into the cultural teaching that debt is just a part of life . . . until it was ruining their lives.

And when it comes to teaching people how to get out of debt, Jade is one of the most passionate people I've ever met.

Jade often co-hosts *The Ramsey Show* with me, she speaks to thousands of people at our events, and she knows what she's talking about because she knows how it feels to be buried under a mountain of debt.

If you're in college (or about to be), Jade will show you how to:

- **Go to college without student loan debt—the greatest financial roadblock for this generation.**
- **Avoid credit cards like the plague.**
- **Start taking college choices seriously—not just where you go and what you study but also things like meal plans and housing.**
- **Live on a budget so you can take control of your money.**
- **Focus on saving money now to get a head start on long-term wealth building.**

I'll be honest with you. The stuff you're about to hear is countercultural. The loudest voices in our society will tell you that you can't go to college without debt, that budgets only steal your joy, and that credit cards let you have everything you want right now with no strings attached. But those are just myths that will bury you for years to come.

We want you to know the truth—and to act on what you know. If you're willing to live out the principles in this book and avoid these five big mistakes, your life will change forever.

YOU WILL EITHER LEARN TO MANAGE **MONEY** OR THE LACK OF IT WILL ALWAYS MANAGE YOU.

— DAVE RAMSEY

STUDENT LOAN DEBT IS NORMAL.
BE DIFFERENT.

MISTAKE NO. ONE
STUDENT LOAN DEBT

STUDENT LOAN

MISTAKE ONE

DEBT

STUDENT LOAN DEBT IS NORMAL.
BE DIFFERENT.

THE AMERICAN STUDENT LOAN CRISIS

It's out of control! Collectively, Americans who have student loans are carrying over $1.7 trillion of student loan debt.[1] That's *trillion* with a capital T!

The average person with student loans leaves college with over $38,000 of federal student loan debt—and even more when it comes to private student loans.[2] That's messed up! And if paying back this debt wasn't a problem for the average American, the government wouldn't constantly use the possibility of student loan forgiveness as a campaign platform.

The fact is, student loans are a huge problem. An eighteen-year-old student can't legally drink alcohol or buy cigarettes, but they can get thousands (hundreds of thousands) of dollars of student loans simply by signing on the dotted line. **In many cases, they receive student loans with no questions, no explanation, and no understanding of the repercussions.** Talk about scary, whacked-out stuff.

That's the first mistake to avoid in college—taking out student loans. You don't have to participate in the madness. You can choose a better way to pay for school that doesn't leave you with a truckload of debt when you graduate. And here's the good news: You can do this!

So, I'm going to give it to you straight because there's no point beating around the bush. **My husband and I came out**

of college with $280,000 of student loan debt. Lord, have mercy—that's a quarter of a million dollars! Now, before you judge me, understand that I was just like you. Sam (that's my husband) was also just like you. And we both felt the pressure . . .

The pressure to take out student loans all begins your junior year of high school when everyone forces you to start thinking about your future. It seems like all the talk is around where you'll go to college and what you'll do with your degree. You want to know which schools have the best "college experience" and which campus is far enough away to have freedom but close enough to fly home for Thanksgiving.

That's fine, but we're forgetting one very important detail . . . I'm talking about money, honey! How much does it cost to go to that school? Who's on the hook for the bill?

> The average person with student loans leaves college with over $38,000 of debt.

My parents told me, "Look, you'd better be smart or good at sports because there ain't no college fund." In other words, **"You're on your own because we aren't planning to pay for your college.** Get a scholarship, get a job, or get a student loan. It's up to you, Jade, to figure out how to pay for this."

Guess what? It's up to you too. You probably feel seen right now because, like me, you have no money saved for college and you're wondering how the heck you're going to make this happen. Or maybe you haven't given it much thought at all. Either way, I'm here to help you sort out all the costly details.

THE AVERAGE COST OF TUITION[3]

PUBLIC TWO-YEAR COMMUNITY COLLEGE
(in-state)
$3,990 per year

PUBLIC FOUR-YEAR COLLEGE/UNIVERSITY
(in-state)
$11,260 per year

PUBLIC FOUR-YEAR COLLEGE/UNIVERSITY
(out-of-state)
$29,150 per year

PRIVATE FOUR-YEAR COLLEGE/UNIVERSITY
$41,540 per year

$0K $5K $10K $15K

IN-STATE AND COMMUNITY COLLEGES CAN SAVE YOU TONS OF MONEY.

AND IT'S ONLY GETTING **HIGHER!**

$25K $30K $35K $40K

DON'T SPEND YOUR FUTURE PAYING FOR YOUR PAST

When it comes to paying for college, there seems to be one big yellow brick road that will take you to the school of your dreams—no matter the cost or location. Ding, ding, ding: Student loans to the rescue. And there are lots of different student loans to choose from, including federal loans, private loans, Parent PLUS Loans, and direct loans.

Culture says, "Don't worry about the details. Just pick a school and a loan. Sign on the dotted line for the golden ticket to your dream school." But I beg to differ. As a matter of fact, I've based my career on helping people avoid debt because I learned the truth—the hard way.

Debt is a thief. It robbed me of my income for nine years because of brutal student loan payments. In total, my student loans were around $34,000, and Sam's had ballooned to around $250,000. **At one point, we were paying almost $2,000 a month in student loan payments!** Don't even get me started on the interest we paid. And back when Sam and I were chipping away at our student loans, there was no such thing as "student loan forgiveness."

Before we knew it, we were two college graduates with music degrees but no real careers, no real prospects, and no real money. **We were on our own with what ended up as $280,000 of student loan debt**—and we only had $30,000 of combined annual income! That math didn't add up.

Think this is uncommon? Think again. **As it stands, nearly 43 million Americans are paying off student loan debt.**[4] The Ramsey Solutions documentary *Borrowed Future* highlights stories similar to ours—and worse. If you haven't watched *Borrowed Future*, take some time to do so. It tells the real truth about the dangers of the student loan industry, including how parents and students get duped into signing up for a lifetime of debt and payments—and the hardship they cause. It's a real eye-opener.

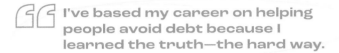

> I've based my career on helping people avoid debt because I learned the truth—the hard way.

The sad thing is, most people have no clue how student loans work. They just follow what everyone believes is the normal path: debt—in the form of student loans. But most students signing up for these loans have little to no idea how the interest and payments on their student loans work—or how fast these stack up. **And they don't understand how long it'll take to pay back their student loans or how difficult those loans will make their lives.**

I hear the excuses all the time. "Not me, Jade. I'm going to be a doctor." Or, "I'm going to be a pharmacist, so my degree will pay for itself in no time." Students throw logic aside and push all their financial chips in on the bet that they'll earn so much money that they'll quickly pay off those student loans. They believe their degree will be worth it, they'll earn back the cost of the degree (and then some!), and finally live happily ever after. Right?

Sorry to burst yet another bubble, but the truth needs to be said: **Debt never reveals its risks or true costs up front. It makes you learn the hard way.**

When you consider how many students drop out and never finish college, end up pursuing different career paths, never pass the LSAT or other exams, or flat out don't earn what they thought they would, reality starts to look straight-up depressing. I don't want that for you.

Here's one thing you should always remember: **Don't spend your future paying for your past.** That means, don't spend the next ten or twenty years paying for your college experience with student loans bills *every* month.

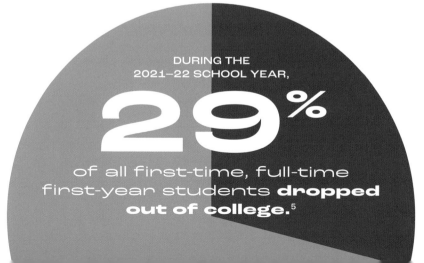

DURING THE
2021–22 SCHOOL YEAR,

29%

of all first-time, full-time first-year students **dropped out of college.**[5]

I OWE $60,000. WITH ALL THE STUDENT LOAN PAYMENTS COMBINED, I PAY $550 EVERY MONTH.

MY BIGGEST REGRET IS THE BURDEN OF MY STUDENT LOAN DEBT.

— JESSE M.

STUDENT LOANS 101

Most students don't have a clue about what student loans are or why they're such a bad option when it comes to paying for college. **Let me be clear: Student loans are a terrible idea!** When you take out student loans, you'll always end up paying a lot more money because of the added interest payments. Interest is the extra money you have to pay for using someone else's money. See an example on pages 13–14.

The bottom line is that any type of student loan (private or federal) is a horrible option for paying for your college expenses. **You'll have debt, and you'll pay back more money than you borrowed in the first place.**

PRIVATE STUDENT LOANS

These loans are funded by a bank, credit union, or school. They typically have higher interest rates, and payments must be made while you're still in school—**not great when you don't have a job**! Since they're privately funded, you're responsible for all of the interest for the entire life of the loan. Ouch!

FEDERAL STUDENT LOANS

These are the most common student loans—**but that doesn't make them okay**. They're funded by the federal government and have a fixed interest rate (it was raised in 2024 to 6.53%).[6] You don't start paying on your loans until six to nine months after you leave school or graduate—the "grace period." *See the info on page 12 for more details on federal student loans.*

TYPES OF FEDERAL STUDENT LOANS

DIRECT SUBSIDIZED

These loans are available to undergraduate students with financial need. Your school determines the amount you can borrow. The federal government subsidizes—or pays for—the interest while you're in school and during the grace period, so you aren't responsible for that part. However, when you start making your payments, interest is then added to your loan amount.

DIRECT UNSUBSIDIZED

These loans are available to undergrads and grad students. There are no financial need requirements. Your school determines the amount you can borrow. The federal government doesn't subsidize—or pay for—the interest on these loans. The interest is added while you're in school and during the grace period. Then that interest is added to your total loan when you start making payments.

DIRECT PLUS LOANS

These loans—Parent PLUS and Grad PLUS—have a higher fixed interest rate (raised to 9.08% in 2024) plus a fee for use.[7] The Parent PLUS Loan is taken out by the parent to cover the cost of attendance. Parents are legally responsible to pay back this loan—and interest accumulates during the life of the loan. The Grad PLUS Loan is for graduate or professional students continuing their education beyond college. Neither of these are great financial options due to the higher interest rate and fees.

These descriptions of student loan options are by no means an endorsement. To be clear: Student loans are a terrible financial option. Avoid them at all costs!

PAYING BACK A STUDENT LOAN IS SO HARD

If you borrow

$38,000

with the current student loan terms

6.53% INTEREST

$432 PER MONTH

10 YEARS OF PAYMENTS

then you'll pay back

$51,848

YEESH.
THAT'S **$13,848** MORE THAN YOU BORROWED.

YOU NEED TO REALIZE THE **LONG-TERM COSTS** OF STUDENT LOANS.

Reality check: If you take out $100,000 in student loans, you'll pay back $1,137 every month for 10 years and end up paying over **$36,000 extra**!

Of course, you could go for the 20-year repayment plan to lower your monthly payment to $747—but after 20 years, you'll pay over **$79,000 extra**!

STIFF-ARM STUDENT LOANS

Okay, okay, enough with the student loan doom and gloom. You may be asking, **"Jade, where's the ray of hope here? Just how am I supposed to pay for school?"** I'm so glad you asked!

Here are some proven, foolproof ways for you to go to college completely debt-free. **You can use one, all, or any combination to make your dreams of a debt-free degree come true.**

CHOOSE THE RIGHT SCHOOL

Sorry, but you shouldn't choose a school based on its football team . . . unless you have a football scholarship. But you *should* choose a school based on location. Say it with me: **"An in-state degree is the degree for me!"**

Don't believe me? **Review the prices for an in-state public college and an out-of-state public college on pages 5–6.** And don't forget to add in the cost for room and board.

Contrary to popular belief, big "name-brand" schools don't equal more job opportunities or higher pay after graduation. You do. *You* are the secret sauce. And here's the truth—no one has ever (ever) asked me where I got my degree before hiring me for a job.

START WITH COMMUNITY COLLEGE

When I was coming up, people made you feel like a loser for considering community college. Now I look back and realize those kids who couldn't care less what others thought are laughing all the way to the bank. Why? **Because they used community college as an affordable way to take their general education classes** and then transferred to another school.

APPLY FOR SCHOLARSHIPS

Instead of assuming you won't win—or not applying because a scholarship is small—just go for it. Apply, apply, apply. **Apply for as many scholarships as you can.** Trust me, the money and the options will add up! I earned several small and two full-ride academic scholarships as well as a volleyball scholarship. But you won't get anything if you don't try.

SAVE UP AHEAD OF TIME

Let me just say, if you have a college fund, what a time to be alive! I'm so happy for you. Now you only have one job: Don't mess this up! If you're blessed enough to have all, or most, of your education paid for, *sweet*. If not, **know that it's not too late to start saving**. You can save a lot of money over summer vacation. Every little bit counts!

WORK AND PAY YOUR WAY THROUGH

In case you haven't been able to put aside all the cash you'll need for college, there's another way to pay in my debt-free bag of tricks. And it involves work. No, not homework (though you'll have plenty). **I'm talking about *work* work, as in getting a J.O.B.** Students who work part time are better managers of their time, less likely to drop out, and have higher GPAs. Research also shows that students who work tend to go on to become higher income earners.[8] That's what I'm talking about!

DON'T GO TO COLLEGE

Stop and hear me out. **Some folks truly don't need the college path to succeed.** Maybe trade school, an apprenticeship, or skill certificates would be a better option. As an entertainer with a commercial music degree, I can tell you—*everything* that I use on a daily basis was learned on the job, in the mix, collaborating and sitting with people. Not in the classroom. If I could go back and do it again, I would choose a different path. Run your race and follow your path to success.

PARENTS DON'T ALWAYS UNDERSTAND

Lastly, don't forget the wise words DJ Jazzy Jeff and the Fresh Prince dropped in their song "Parents Just Don't Understand." I'm not going to hold back here. **Sometimes your parents' advice is the wrong advice.**

Tough love, I know, especially when your parents are the ones suggesting that you take out student loans. Respectfully, they're wrong—even though they want you to get the best education. **The issue is they just don't have all the information.** And that's okay—that's what I'm here for.

One other thing that might sting a little—your parents love you *so* much that they may get their identity a little (or a lot) tied up in yours. Sometimes parents can get entirely too caught up in pedigree or how they'll feel in their friend circle. You may also hear, "Our whole family has attended this university." **Whatever the "thing" is, don't let that be the reason you rack up student loan debt.**

KNOWING WHAT I KNOW NOW, I WOULD **NEVER** SIGN UP FOR STUDENT LOANS.

IT WAS ONE OF THE BIGGEST MISTAKES OF MY LIFE.

— KAYLA B.

GETTING MONEY FOR COLLEGE

I've told you that student loans will put you in debt for many years and that you'll end up paying more than you need to pay for college. **But there are ways to pay for your education without the debt of student loans.** Here are a few ideas:

SCHOLARSHIPS
Scholarships are great because they're free money that doesn't have to be repaid. There are hundreds of scholarships out there. Just do an internet search for "scholarships" to find out what's available, and be prepared to write some essays.

GRANTS
Grants are another form of financial aid that you don't have to pay back. They're funded by schools, organizations, or federal assistance programs. They're based on your financial need and part-time or full-time school status.

WORK-STUDY PROGRAMS
Work-study programs allow students to work part time while attending school. These may be on-campus or off-campus jobs that provide money to help you pay for school.

APPLYING FOR FINANCIAL AID
To apply for any financial aid, you must complete the annual Free Application for Federal Student Aid (FAFSA) by going to the Federal Student Aid site at studentaid.gov. Your school uses this info to determine your eligibility for financial aid.

COMMUNITY COLLEGE

Going to a community college is a great way to get a college education and save some money in the process. Honestly, future employers are more concerned about your final degree than the school name at the top of your diploma. Here are some benefits of community college:

- **Pay lower tuition costs**
- **Attend a smaller campus**
- **Save money by living at home**
- **Have flexibility in class scheduling**
- **Take advantage of online class opportunities**
- **Choose from a variety of programs**
- **Use the latest technologies**
- **Complete your basic requirement classes**
- **Get time to think about what you want to do**
- **Boost your GPA**
- **Specialize in a field of study**
- **Transfer your credits to a university**

DROPPING OUT CAN BE COSTLY

So, what happens to your student loans if you drop out of college? Do they just go away? Nope.

When you sign on the dotted line, you're responsible for paying back that money whether you get your degree or not.

In fact, when you drop out of college, you could end up owing even more money. You'll still have to pay back the money you borrowed with the student loan, and you may also be on the hook for additional costs or fees related to your tuition as well as room and board. **In some cases, you might even have to pay back a portion of any scholarship or grant money you received.** Ouch!

Each school has its own financial rules and policies, so you'll need to check into all of that before you make the decision to drop classes or leave school.

Also, don't forget that dropping out automatically starts your six- or nine-month student loan grace period. And while you won't receive a student loan bill right away, the portion of tuition you owe the school will probably be due immediately.

You may also lose eligibility for any scholarships or grants you've been awarded if you decide to return to school later. **Before dropping out, take a really close look at all of the variables and options.**

If dropping out is a financial decision, you could consider part-time enrollment and pick up a side job. Try to finish the semester so you can at least transfer some credits.

If your school just isn't the right fit for you, check into options for transferring to another school. That's always a better option than just dropping out. If it's a social decision, try getting involved in some on- or off-campus organizations.

Finally—and this is really important—**federal student loans are *not* bankruptable**. That means you can't file bankruptcy to avoid paying back student loans. No matter what, you'll still have to pay back your student loans. They won't go away.

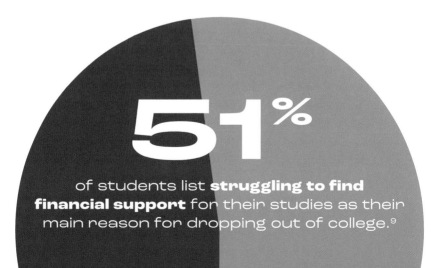

51% of students list **struggling to find financial support** for their studies as their main reason for dropping out of college.[9]

YOU CAN GRADUATE DEBT-FREE

A College Student's Story

by Carrie W.

Before I even learned about Dave Ramsey's financial principles, **I knew I didn't want to experience the stress of student loan debt**. I knew—for my career goals—a college education was vital to securing a good job in an extremely competitive market. I didn't want to feel like I had to take the first job that came along just to pay back my student loans; I wanted to be able to focus on the right job for me.

Lots of people told me not to stress about saving money for college, because student loans would take care of everything. But that's not what I wanted.

> **I know it may seem impossible, but I'm here to tell you that you can get a college degree without student loan debt!**

I wanted to graduate from college debt-free, so with every side gig and summer job, I saved 90% of my paycheck—only keeping 10% for spending money. I applied for more than fifty scholarships and was awarded a handful of those, which covered a huge chunk of my tuition.

Amazon was fantastic when it came to finding textbooks. They typically had affordable prices and free shipping. Amazon also gave me the ability to sell back my books for credit that I could put toward the cost of next semester's books, so **I was able to keep my textbook costs to a minimum**.

I also had some money in savings to help cover my tuition expenses. **I was able to save money by getting a discount when I paid my tuition in full before each semester started.**

Graduating with a four-year degree completely debt-free was extremely liberating! **I know it may seem impossible, but I'm here to tell you that you *can* get a college degree without student loan debt!**

Saving money from work, having support from my mom, and trusting God with my finances were all vital to my success in avoiding student loans. **Also, being cost-effective and mindful of my spending habits was crucial.**

I graduated from college without any debt. Now I have a great job doing something I really enjoy. I can afford to save money and spend it how I choose. That's a great feeling!

. . . .

Carrie W. is a recent college graduate.

MISTAKE NO. TWO   DON'T FALL FOR THE LURES AND
CREDIT CARDS   TRAPS OF CREDIT CARDS

CREDIT

MISTAKE TWO

CARDS

DON'T FALL FOR THE LURES AND TRAPS OF CREDIT CARDS

THE BREAKFAST SANDWICH TRAP

When it comes to college and cash, your decisions will cause you to either sink or swim. For now, I want you to think of me as your lifeguard. **It's my job to protect you from the risky money moves that could seriously cost you during your college years—and long after.**

Before you think it's safe to swim in the water, **I want to tell you about a few sharks that could take a giant bite out of your college experience—and your financial future**. The sharks I'm talking about are credit cards.

The summer after my freshman year of college, I had one successful academic year under my belt, made the dean's list, and scored a new job at S&K Menswear as an associate manager. So I was feeling pretty good! **It was time for me to start thinking ahead about what I needed to do to set my life up financially after graduation.**

I figured credit was important, and since I didn't have any, I'd better find a way to build it. **Without even realizing it, I bought into the lies of using credit cards.** Now, my dad had told me to avoid debt and budget my money. So it seemed like a good idea to just get a *small* credit card and use it *only* for small purchases I could afford and pay off every month. **Little did I know, I was easing myself into a trap.**

There was a McDonald's across from the clothing store where I worked. It just made sense when I stopped for my coffee and bacon, egg, and cheese biscuit to ring that $3.13 up on the ol' credit card. The limit on the card was three hundred bucks, so I wasn't worried. **It would take a lot of breakfast sandwiches to do me in.** Well, that was until there was this trip my friends wanted to take to a theme park in Atlanta. I could use a little of the credit card to help me do more of the things I *wanted*.

> **Without even realizing it, I bought into the lies of using credit cards.**

Once the school year started, my credit card sneaked its way into "helping" me do more things. My boyfriend had a make-or-break interview, and he needed a new suit. Since I worked at a clothing store, I could get a discount! But when the discount still wasn't enough, I just opened a store card. It was my birthday gift to him, and I wanted him to get the job.

In the fall, I *needed* a new coat. I saw a perfect pink peacoat at Express. And they offered 20% off with their store card! That sounded like a great deal to me. Before I knew it, my debt was snowballing. **The thing about credit cards is that you really do feel in control at first.** With names like Freedom and words like *rewards* attached to these cards, they give you a sense of happiness. After a while, I longed for the days of small bacon, egg, and cheese biscuit charges.

Now, I know about credit cards. When I finally counted all of them, I had almost twenty credit cards. *Twenty!* **It was a hot, flaming mess—but it didn't start that way.** I had the best intentions. It's only now, in hindsight, that I see exactly how I got tangled up in that sneaky net of credit card debt.

Listen, credit cards are like a house of cards or a chain of dominoes—all it takes is one to fall and suddenly you can't make your monthly payments. Everything crashes down. **And when you only pay the minimum payment, that compound interest turns damage into devastation.**

And you definitely don't want to miss a payment. That adds additional penalty charges and other fees (that are often hidden in the small print). I'd heard of people getting into credit card trouble, but I never in a million years thought I'd be one of them. I was too smart. And maybe you feel the same way. So, let's play a little game:

- **Raise your hand if you've been told you need to build credit in order to do just about anything.**
- **Raise your hand if you've been told credit cards are a great way to establish credit.**
- **Raise your hand if you've been told credit cards could be a safety net in case of emergencies.**
- **Raise your hand if you've been told credit cards are okay as long as you pay them off every month.**

Here's the thing: I was smart and so are you. But it's not always about intellect. When it comes to credit cards, the playing field isn't exactly level. **Credit card companies spend billions of dollars to find the best way to lure us in.** And it works! Don't fall for it like I did.

DEBT IS DUMB. CASH IS KING. DEBT IS NORMAL. BE WEIRD.

— DAVE RAMSEY

THOSE SNEAKY CREDIT CARD MYTHS

Don't Believe Everything You Hear.

For decades, people have believed the only way to really enjoy life is to rack up piles of debt using a credit card. Wrong! **You can live without the burden of credit card payments.** Just be careful that you don't fall for these six sneaky myths about credit cards.

MYTH: *You need to have a credit card.*
TRUTH: A debit card will do everything a credit card will do—except put you in debt. The best part of using a debit card is that you're only spending money you already have in the bank.

MYTH: *You need a credit card to build your credit score and take advantage of cash-back bonuses and airline miles.*
TRUTH: You don't need a credit score to win with money or build wealth. A high credit score is *not* an indication of winning with money (see pages 35–36).

MYTH: *A credit card is more secure than a debit card.*
TRUTH: If your debit card has a Visa or Mastercard logo on it, you're protected by the exact same protections as the credit card version.[10,11] Yes, that includes if your debit card is lost, stolen, or fraudulently used online or offline.

MYTH: *Credit cards are fun because I can buy whatever I want.*
TRUTH: Debt is anything *but* fun. Your monthly debt payments will eat up most of your income and keep you from enjoying other things in life.

MYTH: *A credit card is good to have in case of emergencies.*
TRUTH: Having at least $500 cash in the bank—an emergency fund—is the best idea for handling life's emergencies. **Cash is always the best option.** The last thing you need in an emergency is to go into debt.

MYTH: *Credit card reward programs are a great benefit.*
TRUTH: Most people spend more with a credit card than they would with cash, and most reward points go unused. Any perks you do earn are wiped away by the extra spending, interest payments, and fees.

CREDIT

While credit cards and debit cards look almost identical, **they are very different**. A little knowledge now can save you a world of heartache—and debt payments—later.

CREDIT CARDS

BORROW AND SPEND MONEY YOU DON'T HAVE

PAY INTEREST ON MONEY YOU DON'T HAVE

BUY AIRLINE TICKETS, RESERVE HOTELS, RENT A CAR

GET PURCHASE AND FRAUD PROTECTION

PAY AN ANNUAL FEE

RACK UP DEBT

CREDIT COMES WITH STRINGS ATTACHED

vs. DEBIT

DEBIT CARDS

SPEND MONEY YOU ALREADY HAVE

DON'T WORRY ABOUT INTEREST OR PAYMENTS

BUY AIRLINE TICKETS, RESERVE HOTELS, RENT A CAR

GET PURCHASE AND FRAUD PROTECTION

USE FOR FREE

ENJOY DEBT-FREE SPENDING

The bottom line: When you use a credit card, you're borrowing money and going into debt to buy something. **When you use a debit card, you're using your money to buy the things you want**—and you don't have to make payments on it later. When you make payments, there will be interest—which makes everything cost so much more.

THE FICO TRUTH

When most people think of a credit score, they often think of the FICO score because that's the one you hear mentioned on TV. The FICO score, named after the company that computes credit scores, is just one of the ways credit scores are measured. Other companies, such as Equifax, TransUnion, and Experian, also compute credit scores.

Here's the shocker: **According to FICO's website, 100% of your score is based on your debt, not your wealth.** It has nothing to do with your savings, your income, or your investments.

> At the end of the day, the FICO score is just an "I love debt" score.

What's really amazing is that you could inherit $1 million tomorrow from some relative and it would not change your credit score one bit—even though you'd be a millionaire!

The credit score is not a measure of winning financially. A high credit score just means that you have debt, use debt, and love debt. **At the end of the day, the FICO score is just an "I love debt" score.**

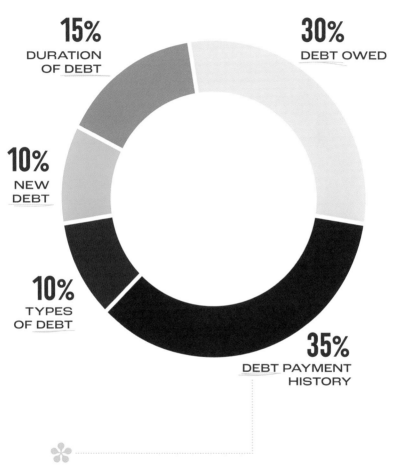

15%
DURATION
OF DEBT

30%
DEBT OWED

10%
NEW
DEBT

10%
TYPES
OF DEBT

35%
DEBT PAYMENT
HISTORY

Reality check: Having no credit score is not a bad thing—it shows you don't feel the need to keep yourself in debt. A high credit score doesn't mean you know how to handle money. It just shows you've used lots of debt.

A WORLD OF
LURES AND TRAPS

Here's the thing: Credit cards are not designed to trap us intellectually. **Credit cards are designed to trap us emotionally.** Companies spend billions of dollars finding the best ways to lure us in through emotion and psychology. And guess what—those lures and traps work!

As it stands today, Americans have over $1 *trillion* of credit card debt.[13] For those of you majoring in math, you know that's a lot of zeros (twelve to be exact). And the average American with credit cards is carrying a revolving debt of around $6,000 each month—meaning the debt isn't getting paid off each month.[14] In fact, less than half of all people pay off their credit card each month.[15]

Not to mention that the interest rates for using credit cards are astronomical. **Today, the average interest rate for credit cards is around 22%!**[16] And do you know where you find that information? In the teeny tiny print on the agreement form you use to sign up.

Here's what that looks like in real numbers: If you spend $100 buying a new outfit on your credit card, they can add $22 to your total bill—making it $122 if you don't pay it on time and in full. And since the interest is compounding, the next month they can now charge you 22% of $122 (not just the original $100), which means they can add another $26.84 to your bill, bringing it to $148.84 if you don't pay on time and in full. That amount doesn't include late fees or overbalance charges. **You don't even have to be a big spender or irresponsible for things to get out of control fast!** It just takes a couple of months of missing payments, or just making minimum payments, to let things spiral out of control. It happened to me—and I guarantee that if you throw a rock, you'll hit someone who is currently in credit card debt too.

Americans have over $1,000,000,000,000 of credit card debt.

And while we're talking about lures and traps, another big one (though not a credit card, but it does involve credit and debt) is a car loan. You may think you need to buy a brand-new car— and you need a loan to do it. **But that's the most expensive way to buy a car.** Period. Don't fall for this trap.

First of all, that brand-new car will lose a huge chunk of value the moment you drive it off the car lot. Seriously. A new car will lose 60% of its value in the first five years.[17] That means you'll owe more on the car than it's worth!

Take it from me, credit card companies (and car loans) are not your friends, and they don't want to help you win financially. They're designed to make money off of you. All they want is for you to buy more, miss payments, accumulate interest, and pay more over time. **They offer "points" and "rewards" to trick you into doing it.** That's how they make money—and they're great at it.

YOU NEED TO BUY THIS THING

There are many different things you can buy—in stores and online—but you only have so much money. **That means you can't buy everything, even if you wanted to.**

Companies know this. So they spend a lot of money on marketing, and they study the spending habits of college students. Based on the results, they create TV, radio, and even social media ads targeted directly to you. **With the amount of time you spend online, it's safe to say that you're exposed to thousands of advertisements each day.**

Now, advertising and marketing aren't evil, but you do have to be careful. **The most effective ads target *your* wants and needs and make you feel as though companies really care about you.** But really, most of those companies are just trying to get you to buy their stuff.

Marketing is all around you. Names, logos, and labels are on everything. You probably have several logos within eyeshot right now. These names and labels generate brand loyalty—and that's why so much money is spent on advertising.

Companies also spend a lot of money buying the best shelf spaces at your favorite stores. And they pay for product placement so specific brands show up in the hands of your favorite actors in your favorite movies. The results of those marketing plans can be seen in the things we buy.

HOW COLLEGE STUDENTS SPEND THEIR MONEY

Beyond the cost of tuition, room and board, books, and school fees, college students spend their money on personal things too. Here are the top categories:[18]

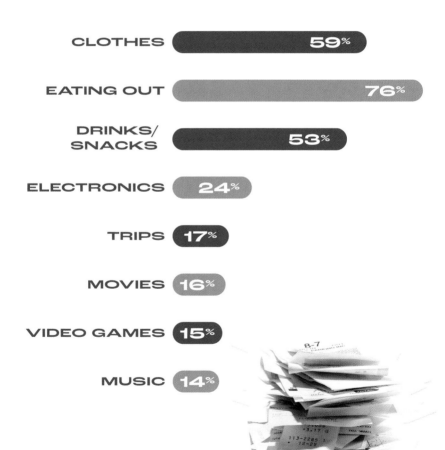

Category	Percentage
CLOTHES	59%
EATING OUT	76%
DRINKS/SNACKS	53%
ELECTRONICS	24%
TRIPS	17%
MOVIES	16%
VIDEO GAMES	15%
MUSIC	14%

BREAK UP WITH CREDIT CARDS

Now that you know the facts, let's get into it. **I'm going to show you how to cut ties with credit cards** and live your life without using them as a crutch.

1. **Save cash for emergencies.**

   A lot of times, people think credit cards are the answer when their cash can't cut it. **But what if you saved up enough cash so that your cash could, in fact, cut it?** Wow! I just blew your mind. Saving up $500 would be enough to cover a flat tire or many other unexpected, urgent, and necessary expenses.

   The key word is *necessary.* That doesn't include buying a ticket to Beyonce's tour. And it definitely doesn't include taking your girl out to a fancy restaurant! **Having a $500 emergency fund is just the cushion you need between you and life.** That peace of mind will help you enjoy more important things, like finding the best tacos near campus.

   Here are four fast ways to save up your emergency fund:
   - **Increase your income.** Go get this money! Sell some of your stuff, start a side hustle, get a summer job, cut back on spending. Do whatever it takes—as long as it's fast and legal!
   - **Budget for savings.** Maybe you already have a decent amount of money coming in. If that's the case, it's as simple as budgeting some of your income to set aside.
   - **Keep your savings separate.** Why is your money sitting in a pile where you can see it tempting you? Put it

somewhere safe where it's not so noticeable. An online savings account separate from your usual checking account is a great place. That way, you won't see it every day, and you wont "accidentally" spend it.

- **Set it and forget it!** Now more than ever, you need to use your good judgment. That $500 is for emergencies *only*. Don't let Amazon convince you otherwise (Amazon is *not* an emergency).

2. **Declare war on debt.**
   All right! I feel like we've really bonded here. It's almost like we're best friends. And as best friends, I need to let you know that the second key to cutting ties with credit cards is to declare war on debt. Just decide it's not something you need or want in your life. **As your best friend, I'm telling you that you don't need debt or credit cards—but they need you!** You hold all the power, my friend, because you hold the money. And now, you've decided you aren't giving your money away in debt payments to a credit card company. Good for you!

3. **Give yourself credit.**
   I'm talking about taking credit because you're able to pay for what you need without borrowing money—especially in the form of debt on a credit card. But there's one slightly large, very confused-looking elephant in the room that we need to deal with. "So, best friend, older sister Jade— how am I supposed to build my credit if I don't use debt and credit cards?" The answer is simple: You don't! Keep reading on the next page and let me explain.

The whole point of building credit is so you can borrow more money. But when you use the money that you have instead of borrowing it, guess what? **You won't go into debt, which means you don't need credit (or a credit card).** Put another way: **When you don't have debt, you have money.** You simply buy what you need. It turns out, the whole idea of borrowing money to build credit is just a bad plan meant to throw you off track.

And hear me out: Down the road, you may want to do things that you've been told you need credit to do, like rent an apartment. Again, anyone telling you credit is the only way to rent an apartment is wrong. You just need to find the right apartment. **It's absolutely possible to rent an apartment without a credit score.** You may have to pay a higher deposit, but it can be done—and it's worth it.

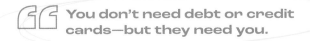 **You don't need debt or credit cards—but they need you.**

Wow! We really covered a lot, and we've grown much closer along the way. I hope you know how much I care about you and your financial and academic future. **You're getting ready to step into one of the most exciting times of your life.** The fact that you're even reading this book means you're quite the responsible adult. Well done.

It's a great privilege for me to speak into your life. And if you decide to stay with me just a little longer, I'd be so honored. **I want to unpack a few more areas that could save you a lot of heartache and money along your collegiate journey.**

I'VE NEVER OWNED A CREDIT CARD. PAYING IN **CASH** GIVES ME A VISUAL OF AN ITEM'S VALUE.

— JOHN S.

03

MISTAKE NO. THREE
DUMB CHOICES

KNOWING BETTER MEANS
YOU'LL DO BETTER.

DUMB

MISTAKE THREE

CHOICES

KNOWING BETTER MEANS
YOU'LL DO BETTER.

REAL TALK AND DUMB CHOICES

Fact: You're getting ready to enter a completely new and exciting chapter in life. You're probably feeling a whirlwind of emotions. I remember feeling everything from excitement and anticipation to sheer terror. **This is the moment you've waited for—to strike out on your own, set your own course, and make your own choices.** But the reality is, going off to college may be your first experience being on your own in the "real world." So hold on!

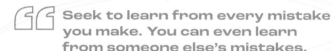

> **Seek to learn from every mistake you make. You can even learn from someone else's mistakes.**

As excited and confident as you may feel at certain moments, there's probably also a part of you that knows you'll make mistakes along the way. **Listen: Don't fear the mistakes you could make—instead, fear not learning from them.** College is all about higher learning right? Well, that doesn't just apply to your studies. It also applies to your decisions, so seek to learn from every mistake you make. You can even learn from someone else's mistakes. (Let one of those someones be me. Lord! I've made some mistakes.)

To be honest and totally real with you, I'm pretty sure it's nearly impossible to go through college without making some bad, irresponsible, and just dumb choices. And you're supposed to make dumb choices! It's how you learn.

I'd like you to consider the idea that there are two types of dumb choices—those you're warned about (and choose to do anyway) and the ones you make because you had no idea it was dumb and didn't see it coming. Both are great learning experiences. But if you're going to make a dumb choice—and you will—aim for the second type.

One of my favorite quotes about making choices comes from Maya Angelou. She says, **"Do the best you can until you know better. Then when you know better, do better."** And another comes from Warren Buffett: "It's good to learn from your mistakes. It's better to learn from other people's mistakes."

I want to help you avoid making dumb choices by giving you the chance to learn from mine. You're about to make some big decisions that could rock your money world, big time. I'm talking about everything from choosing a major to selecting your housing, food, and book options—and don't forget buying a car. It's so important that you make smart spending choices here.

75%

of students say they
are moderately, slightly,
or **not prepared at all**
to go to college.[19]

CHOOSING YOUR MAJOR

Some students go to college knowing exactly what they want to do for a career. But many enter college undecided about a major. That's okay. **The reality is that many students change their major during the first two years.** You'll be taking a lot of basic classes during that time anyway. And there's nothing wrong with changing your major.

But locking in a major by the end of your first or second year is a big deal because it will determine a majority of the classes you'll need to take from then on. It really is one of the most important choices you'll make in college. Here are five ideas to help you choose your major:

CONSIDER YOUR INTERESTS AND PASSIONS
What do you really enjoy? What's your passion? What topics or subjects interest you? If your major is something you really enjoy, you'll be more likely to study and go to class.

EXPLORE SOME OPTIONS
If you aren't sure what you want to study, list your major as *undeclared.* That won't lock you into any set plan. During your first few semesters, try several fields of study to see what clicks. Get input from other students and guidance counselors too.

CONSIDER THE COST

Don't spend $100,000 getting a college degree for a job that will only pay you $35,000 per year. But don't let a salary be the only factor in choosing your career. Keep in mind that no amount of money can make you enjoy a job you absolutely hate!

EXAMINE THE JOB OPTIONS

Make sure there are jobs in demand for the major you choose. Also, a major that provides several options is better than a major that only gives you one career choice. You don't want to spend four years in school and then not be able to get a job.

SHADOW SOMEONE FOR A DAY

Follow someone in your intended career field for a day or two to see what kinds of things they do—and if you would enjoy it. It's better to find out what you like or don't like before you get too far down the requirements for your major.

Don't rush your decision. Spend some time discovering your best choice for a major. **Don't pick a major just because your best friend did or because you can make a bunch of money once you graduate and have a career.** Your major should be a reflection of who you are and what interests you.

SAVE CASH, GET COLLEGE CREDIT

Did you know there are several ways you can save on the cost of your tuition? There are. And sometimes you can even earn college credit at the same time.

CLEP TESTS

College-Level Examination Program (CLEP) tests offer you the opportunity to earn a qualifying test score on over thirty college subject tests. **That means doing well on a single test could allow you to skip some college courses, which saves you tuition money!**

You can find tests in subjects that you may already know quite a bit about. This is a relatively painless way to test out of some college courses—especially prerequisite courses.

The tests typically cost less than $100 to take, so you can earn college credits for a lot less than you would pay per credit hour at your college. Check with your college to see if they accept CLEP tests, what score you would need on the test to receive credit, and how many credit hours you could earn with CLEP testing.

For more information on CLEP testing, check out clep.collegeboard.org.

INTERNSHIPS

Internships are another way to earn college credit hours and gain valuable work experience in the process. **Don't underestimate the positive impact that an internship will have on your resumé.**

A paid internship may be hard to find, but earning college credit is the main goal. If you do get paid, put that money back into your class costs. Check with your college regarding the guidelines—and costs—related to internships.

Another benefit of internships is that they allow you to try a career field to find out if it's the right fit for you. For example, if you're interested in medical or nursing school, working in a hospital is a good first step. If you discover that the sight of blood makes you queasy, you've just saved yourself a bunch of time and money.

Internships also connect you with experienced people who can mentor you and give you a great professional reference later. You might even intern for a company that ends up hiring you full time out of college!

PEER LEADERSHIP

Becoming an RA (resident assistant) often comes with free or discounted room and board. This is a fantastic way to trim a huge chunk of your college expenses. But most schools won't let you become an RA until you've completed your freshman year, so check out the rules at your school.

SAVING

Going away to college can be exciting—**but it's also very expensive!** Some of the biggest expenses are room and board (where you're going to live and what you're going to eat) and books. Here's a closer look—as well as some ideas to save money.

HOUSING

AVERAGE COST: **$8,173—9,376** [20,21]

- **Live at home and commute.**
- **Live off campus with roommates.**
- **Be an RA (resident assistant).**
- **Choose a less expensive dorm.**

SMART CHOICES CAN SAVE YOU BIG MONEY ON COLLEGE COSTS.

MONEY

EATING

AVERAGE COST: **$4,597–5,274** [22,23]

- Eat at home.
- Buy a less expensive meal plan.
- Live off campus and buy your own food.
- Pack a lunch and snacks.

BOOKS

AVERAGE COST: **$1,250** [24]

- Buy used books.
- Buy e-books.
- Borrow or rent books.
- Check the library.

MAKING IT COUNT

Before you know it, you'll wake up and be twenty-five years old. Don't become that person who looks back on their college days with a pile of regret because of the decisions they made in college.

Every decision you make today will have consequences—positive or negative—on your future. Here are some choices and wisdom you'll be thankful for several years from now.

BUILD QUALITY RELATIONSHIPS
A handful of really good friends will become more important than a bunch of mediocre relationships.

STAY OUT OF DEBT
Your post-college budget will thank you for not having a mountain of debt payments that eat up your paycheck.

PURSUE YOUR PASSIONS
Turning your passions into a paying career is always a bonus. You'll make money and enjoy what you're doing.

UNDERSTAND THE IMPORTANCE OF INSURANCE
Renters, health, and auto insurances will protect you and your money. Sure, they cost money, but if you ever need them, you'll be glad you have them.

EMBRACE CHANGE

No matter how good or bad things may be, you can always count on change. Being able to adapt to change will help you in the long run.

RECOGNIZE THE POWER OF COMPOUND INTEREST

Compound interest is the interest you earn from the original amount (or principal) of an investment plus any interest you've already made through that investment. **Your investments need two things to make you a millionaire: money invested and time to grow.** So start investing as early as you can!

BELIEVE IN YOURSELF

Have confidence in yourself and what you can do. Don't let anyone else tell you who or what you should be. *You* are the secret to what you can accomplish and earn in life.

BE CAUTIOUS ONLINE

Anything you post online becomes part of your digital footprint. Things online live forever, so be smart with what you post. It will follow you everywhere.

TAKE CARE OF YOURSELF

If healthy eating and exercise aren't a normal part of your life already, now is the perfect time to make that change. You'll not only create good habits that will keep you strong and healthy for life, but you'll also have more energy to do the things you want to do today.

SAVVY SPENDING

When it's time to make a purchase, especially a large one, always stop and think about it. Seriously. Take a breath. **Don't give in to impulse purchases**—seeing something you think you can't live without and buying it right then and there.

I've found that it's always a good idea to do some research before you make a large purchase. Of course, the internet is a great resource when it comes time to find information. Just remember: **You can't believe everything you read online.**

But when it comes to product reviews, the internet can be a big help in making wise purchases. Just search for reviews to see what others have to say. Be careful, though, because a lot of what you find online is actually marketing disguised as product reviews. **Find a few reputable sources you like and stick to them.**

As a smart consumer, you want to see what actual owners have to say about whatever you're interested in. **When it comes to reviews, 99.5% of shoppers read reviews, with the most popular reviews being on Amazon (94%), retail sites (91%), search engines (70%), and brand sites (68%).**[25]

As long as you look on reputable sites, you should be able to find reviews you can use to make decisions. If you don't feel comfortable about a product after reading what actual owners of that product think, don't buy it.

Another thing I've learned to do is wait a day or two before making a larger purchase. Sometimes we get so excited about buying something that we rush into a dumb decision. You can usually avoid that by waiting overnight. If it still seems like a good idea the next day and you can afford it, go for it.

Finally, make sure you can pay cash for the purchase. One of my favorite sayings is, "Getting control of your money is a way to love yourself, your family, and your future well." Debt is not good for you, now or in the future.

One of the best ways to control your spending is to use cash! Why? Because the greatest purchase is a debt-free purchase. **It's always a bad idea to go into debt for a purchase.**

Here's one last piece of advice: **If you don't have the cash, you can't afford it.**

$1,812
The average amount of money people spend on **impulse purchases** every year.[26]

I BOUGHT A CAR— THE WRONG WAY!

Let me share an example of a time when I made a pretty dumb mistake (okay, multiple mistakes) that I easily could have avoided. I definitely learned from them, and I hope you'll learn from my ridiculousness. Real talk: I was a stellar student. I made great grades and was on the dean's list the majority of my semesters in college.

I mentioned earlier that I had a full-ride scholarship. I was an athlete on the volleyball team, responsible with my time, and my dad worked on campus in college admissions. I had advisors and smart people all around me. I was set up to win! Yet I had this genius idea that I needed a car.

If you're thinking, *Needing a car isn't so bad. What's the catch?* I'll tell you the catch. **I thought it would be a great idea to take out student loans and use that money to buy a car!** That was a dumb decision, and here's why: I didn't have to pay for school (thanks to scholarships), so I didn't need student loans in the first place. But my financial aid advisor suggested loans as a way to fund my lifestyle, so I signed up.

I thought that using financial aid was the same as paying cash for a car. **I had the right motivation but the wrong course of action and the wrong context. It was all wrong.**

The year was 2003, and the car I liked was a very used, dull brown 1996 Ford Taurus—but it had beige leather seats and electric windows. It was $5,000 and I loved it!

I thought I had hit it big. Especially since I previously had my eye on a $3,000 car that my dad convinced me wouldn't be reliable. He encouraged me to set my sights higher, which is why I went with the Taurus. Spoiler alert: **That car gave me more trouble than a defendant on Judge Judy.** It was not reliable. At. All.

> **I thought it would be a great idea to take out student loans and use that money to buy a car!**

Now , I knew I didn't want a car payment. I wanted to buy the car outright. I told my dad this, and he thought it was great. **But he didn't know I was using a student loan to buy the car. I told him I had saved up the money.** And in my head, I thought that was true. It was leftover student loan money that was just sitting in my student account, that I had "saved" by not spending it. I'd heard it was smart to pay cash for cars, and in my mind, technically, I did pay cash for the car—using the money from taking out a student loan.

I truly didn't realize it was different from cash earned at, say, a job. **I was using debt to buy my car. Even though the debt wasn't coming from a car dealership, it was still car debt!** I knew the money would need to be paid back, but I figured it was fine to add it to my existing debt. I thought I was making a smart choice. In reality, I was making a dumb choice—a really dumb choice.

GOAL: PAY CASH FOR A CAR

Yes, friend, pay cash for a car—but don't use student loans or other debt like I did. I'm talking about actual cash. As in get a job and save up the money. When it comes to buying a good, used car, $5,000 isn't a bad place to start. You might spend a little more or a little less. **I'm happy with whatever it costs—as long as you pay for your car in full, with cash.**

As it stands, **the average new-car payment in the United States is $729 per month.**[27] Are you kidding me? Maybe $729 sounds normal because your friends or parents have similar car loans. **But let me be the one to tell you—a car payment is the trap that keeps most Americans in debt for life because we call it "normal."** After all, you need a car to get to work, right? But the reality is, most people have no idea how much that car payment actually costs them. Yes, you need a car—but you don't need a car payment to have one.

When you finance a car, you end up paying way more for it. Financing means you borrow the full amount from a bank and then pay it all back with interest in monthly installments. Right now, the average interest rate for a used car is around 8%, and the average term to pay it back is about five years.

So, let's say you were to finance a $20,000 car. **After five years and 8.76% interest, that $20,000 car would actually cost you $24,770.** Yeesh! Not only did you pay almost $5,000 more, you were strapped with a $413 payment every month for half a decade. No thank you!

Here's something that most people somehow forget when it comes to buying a car: **Anytime you make payments of any kind, you rob from your ability to focus on what really matters financially.**

Right now, rather than having your money snapped up by car payments, **you should be focused on saving $500 for emergencies,** paying cash for any tuition costs, and then saving up to pay cash for a car. In the future, you can save your money to do things like move into an apartment or go on a spring break trip with your friends.

> **A car payment is the trap that keeps most Americans in debt for life because we call it "normal."**

Do you remember my dumb choice when it came to buying a car? Yep, that left a scar—and I want to keep you from making the same decision. Are you following me? **You can learn from my mistake now—or make your own mistake that you'll regret later.** Choose wisely!

At this point, I hope you agree with me: **It's a mistake to take out debt to buy a car, especially a brand-new car.** The best way to buy a car is simply to commit to cash—because using cash gives you freedom and no debt.

The last thing you want to be worried about in school is making a car payment. You have way more important things to worry about—like your grades, where you're going for spring break, or what's on the menu today.

THE REAL WORLD

Thoughts from College Students

In my first semester, I was too focused on friends and my social life—and not focused enough on school. I ended up failing that semester. It took a lot of hard work to get my GPA up from a 1.0 to the 3.6 I graduated with. — Alison B.

My biggest regret was my time-management skills. I also wish I had been more proactive with my assignments. — Daniel W.

I remember the monumental anxiety I had over so many things: class registration, essay due dates, finals, and other stuff. If I'd taken it all seriously, I would have had an easier time managing the stress levels. — Rebecca J.

The most significant regret I have is the major I chose. I didn't have adequate information at the age of eighteen to make an intelligent decision about my career path. — Colby M.

I wish someone had told me to keep in touch with the best friends you meet in college. Life will take you in different directions. I wish I had known to cherish those friendships when they were with me. — Kristen M.

The most helpful advice I received was to get involved in campus organizations. I got to take on leadership roles and really come out of my shell. — Melissa W.

I WISH I WOULD HAVE KNOWN THAT **COLLEGE** WASN'T GOING TO BE LIKE HIGH SCHOOL.

IT REQUIRED A LOT MORE RESPONSIBILITY THAN I EXPECTED.

— ROBERT P.

MISTAKE NUMBER | THE GRADUATE SURVIVAL GUIDE |

04

A BUDGET DOESN'T CONFINE YOUR MONEY,
IT DEFINES YOUR MONEY.

MISTAKE NO. FOUR
NO PLAN

NO

MISTAKE FOUR

PLAN

A BUDGET DOESN'T CONFINE YOUR MONEY,
IT DEFINES YOUR MONEY.

A PLAN FOR YOUR MONEY

At this point, you might be thinking, *That's a lot of money stuff to manage! How do I juggle all of this on top of my normal day-to-day or month-to-month spending? It's almost like I need a way to keep track of all of this stuff. It's almost like I need a written plan of some sort that I can refer to daily if needed.*

Exactly! **The good news is that I have just the plan for you—and it's called a budget.**

You know how in the movies when a DJ is playing music and something awkward happens, the music suddenly screeches to a halt? I feel like that's what just happened. **I know what you might be thinking: *A budget doesn't exactly sound like a lot of fun.*** Typically, the words *budget* and *college experience* aren't used together. When most people hear *college experience* they think:

> College + Study
> College + Party
> College + Football

Nobody thinks: College + Budget. That probably just leaves you feeling confused. Hey—I get it! **When I was growing up, *budget* was basically a curse word in our house.** So I developed a pretty negative view of budgeting.

As a college student, I had a part-time job and probably could have done much better in planning how to spend my money. Instead, I just wasted my money. I can't even say exactly where it all went. I let those negative thoughts about budgeting follow me all the way through college and into my young adulthood. **I wasted so much time when I could have been making a plan for my money!**

 A budget is simply a plan for your money. That's it. It's a way to decide how *you* want to spend *your* money each month.

But back then, I didn't understand that a budget is the most effective way to manage your money. Here are some of the messed-up lies I believed back then:

1. **I thought a budget was something that restricted you from spending.**
   I truly thought using a budget meant you weren't allowed to spend money on anything fun. It meant your money would only go to pay bills.

2. **I thought budgets were for poor people.**
   When I was a kid, we weren't poor, but we weren't exactly rich either. The only context I heard about budgets seemed to be around people who didn't have enough money to spend whatever they wanted, whenever they wanted.

3. **I thought budgets weren't for students.**
   Isn't college supposed to be the "treat yourself" era—or a time when you don't have a care in the world? Especially cares about money and the things you want to buy!

4. **I thought a budget was just a list of your debts.**
   I had this idea that budgeting was just a list of all the money you owed to people. And that's it. No fun, no extra, and no changes. No thanks!

5. **I thought a budget was some kind of punishment.**
   Finally, I viewed a budget as punishment for all the things I listed above. If you had a budget, it was your punishment for being poor, bad with money, and having debt.

Wow, was I wrong! But thankfully, I've grown since then, and now I know the truth: **A budget is simply a plan for your money.** That's it. It's a way to decide how *you* want to spend *your* money each month. Period. No drama. No punishment.

Once I started budgeting for myself, I realized budgeting is actually pretty awesome—it's like a financial super power. **Because once you have control of your money, it feels like you have more of it.** It's almost like getting a pay increase!

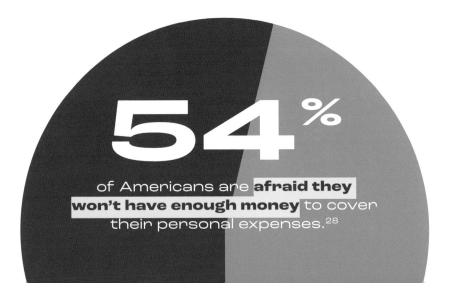

54% of Americans are **afraid they won't have enough money** to cover their personal expenses.[28]

BUDGETING IS SELF-CARE. IT'S DECIDING THAT YOUR SELF CARES ABOUT **WHERE** YOUR MONEY GOES!

— JADE WARSHAW

FIVE TRUTHS ABOUT BUDGETS

1. **A budget is custom organization for your money.**
   Picture Kim Kardashian's closet. Each purse and shoe has its own compartment, there's attention to detail, and every item is taken care of. There's a space for everything, and everything is in its space. And it all functions to meet *her* needs. **The same is true about a good budget—you're creating custom organization for every one of your dollars.** No cash just haphazardly heaped in a corner. You're assigning a compartment or purpose for every dollar.

2. **A budget doesn't confine your money—it defines it.**
   Contrary to what I thought as a child, budgets don't keep you from spending. **You simply decide ahead of time what you're going to spend your money on.** Simple as that. It's your money and it's your plan. A budget just gives each dollar a specific job to do. That's all! As Ramsey Personality Rachel Cruze says, "A budget gives you permission to spend!"

3. **A budget is like a toothbrush—everyone needs one.**
   If you think you can get through life without a plan for your money, you're playing yourself. Everyone needs a budget. Why? Because until you're a squillionaire, your income has limitations. **You can't just spend without boundaries.** If you try to, I guarantee things will get ugly real quick! The same way all people need a toothbrush to maintain daily healthy hygiene, budgets are a tool everyone needs to maintain daily financial hygiene. Learning to check in with

your money on a daily basis, whether opening your budget app or checking your account balance, is a great way to keep your money minty fresh.

4. **A budget is a map that leads to all your money goals.**
A budget doesn't just help you pay your monthly cell phone bill on time and plan your extra going-out spending money for the weekends. It also helps you strategize for your long-term goals, like saving up for an apartment and buying the furniture to deck it out. **A good budget allows you to plan for your life today while keeping in mind what you want your life to look like in the future.** The budget is where you're able to put aside money to do the things that truly set you up for the good life. That includes things like saving for emergencies, buying cars in cash, and even buying a house and investing for the future.

5. **Budgets aren't for people who have no money. They're for people who *refuse* to have no money.**
After fifteen solid years of budgeting for myself, I can tell you that budgets are not simply for poor people who have no money. They're for anyone who refuses to feel the stress and strain of living paycheck to paycheck. They're for people who want peace and control around their money. **They're for people who understand they work too hard to feel like they ain't got no money.**

BUDGETING 101

A budget is just a written plan for your money. It doesn't have to be fancy or complicated. But if you live without a budget, you'll get to the end of the month and have no idea where all your hard-earned money went. **Author John Maxwell puts it simply: "A budget is telling your money where to go instead of wondering where it went."**

To win with money, you need a zero-based budget every month. That just means you're planning out all of your spending ahead of time so your income minus your expenses equals zero. But that doesn't mean you're spending every dollar you earn! You're just giving every dollar a job to do—whether that's giving, saving, or spending.

Here's how it's done: Start by listing all of your sources of income for the month. This includes paychecks from work or side jobs, financial support from family, and any other money.

Next, list every expense you have for the month. This includes school fees, food, rent, clothing, gas, bills, savings, entertainment—everything! Do this every month because your budget will change depending on what's going on each month.

Remember: You're the boss of your budget. **Once you've set your budget, stick to it.** Don't get discouraged if the first month is a little bumpy. It usually takes about three months to get the hang of it. On the next page, you'll see what a sample budget for a typical college freshman might look like.

BUDGET FOR THIS MONTH

INCOME

Paychecks from Work	$ 1,200
Support from Parents	$ 200
Side Job	$ 400
Total =	**$ 1,800**

EXPENSES

Giving	$ 180
Food	$ 60
Rent	$ 345
Gas	$ 75
Car Insurance	$ 70
School Fees/Supplies	$ 100
Entertainment	$ 50
Restaurants	$ 50
Personal Spending Money	$ 20
Road Trips/Weekends Home	$ 50
Savings for Tuition	$ 500
Savings for Emergencies	$ 50
Savings for My Next Car	$ 250
Total =	**$ 1,800**

TOTAL

Income	$ 1,800
Expenses	- $ 1,800

$0

MAKING

If the "poor college student" lifestyle is a reality for you, then finding some ways to make extra money may be at the top of your to-do list. The best way to make money is by going to work. Yes, work. A recent study showed that 42% of full-time college students have jobs, and 81% of part-time college students work.[29]

COLLEGE STUDENTS WITH JOBS

NOT EVERYONE'S AT THE PARTY

42% full-time students

81% part-time students

0%   50%   100%

THERE'S A GREAT PLACE TO GO WHEN YOU'RE BROKE—TO WORK.

MONEY

Here are some ways to make money while you're in college:

GET AN ON-CAMPUS JOB
Most will pay minimum wage.

DELIVER FOOD
You could make an average of $19 per hour.[30]

BECOME A BARISTA
You could make an average of around $15 an hour.[31]

APPLY FOR SCHOLARSHIPS
Sure, you have to write some essays, but it's totally worth your time.

WALK DOGS
You could make an average of around $18.50 an hour.[32]

RUN ERRANDS
You could make an average of about $15 per hour.[33]

OFFER TUTORING
You could make an average of about $24 an hour.[34]

WORK RETAIL
Retail jobs are easy to find, and most employers will work around class schedules. You could make an average of over $15 an hour.[35]

FLEX YOUR BUDGET MUSCLE

The majority of Americans live paycheck to paycheck. This means that the money they have totally runs out before the month ends or they barely squeak by to the next payday. **Living paycheck to paycheck means you have no breathing room with your money.** Instead, you're spending everything you get, and by the end of the month, there's no money left to do responsible things like save or give. Or you only have enough money to pay the bills and maybe a few other things, but there's no margin or extra money. Now that's frustrating!

I talk to people all the time who tell me they can't remember what they spent money on the month before. It's no wonder they're living paycheck to paycheck. Without a plan, it's easy for your money to disappear.

All it takes is spending an extra $25 here at your favorite clothing store or $15 there on a quick pick-me-up at your favorite fast-food place each week to blow through $100! Is there a connection here? I think yes!

When you don't have a plan for what you can spend and when you can spend it, it's easy to spend impulsively and go overboard with your purchases. Especially at certain times of the year. Football season can get hectic with games and activities taking place each weekend. Not only can all that unplanned spending eat up all your margin, but it can cut into the money you need to cover actual expenses, like rent, cell phone bills, and other responsibilities. Oops! Time to call your parents to ask them for a few bucks—but not on your iPhone, because the line's been cut off. Looks like you'll have to use your roommate's Android. Yikes!

Now, don't get me wrong, I want you to spend some money and have a good time, but I also want you to be smart and intentional. **Remember, college is all about learning— and learning how to properly manage your money is no exception.** I want you to control your money instead of a lack of money controlling you.

 When you don't have a plan for what you can spend and when you can spend it, it's easy to spend impulsively and go overboard.

The truth is, budgeting is self-care. It's deciding that your self cares about your money! And just like you go to the gym to take care of your physical fitness as an act of self-care, **starting a healthy habit of budgeting early is one of the best things you will ever do for your financial fitness**.

When you choose to become a budgeter, you're simply saying, "I care about how I spend my hard-earned money. I have goals, and I have the power to accomplish them." **The more you practice budgeting, the better you'll get at it** and the stronger you'll become financially. That's real financial fitness.

So, what's the best way to budget? Don't worry, I have all the intel on that too! **The best way to budget is using an app called EveryDollar.** It's free, and you can use it on your phone so your budget is always with you. There's also a desktop version. I've even included a QR code to help you get started with EveryDollar. Check it out. **I love using EveryDollar!**

Inside EveryDollar, you can do all the things we've talked about. You can list all the money you have coming in this month (your income), and then you'll subtract all the things you want or need to spend money on this month (your expenses). **Keep subtracting your expenses from your income until the final dollar amount hits zero.** That's called a zero-based budget—because you're giving each dollar an assignment for the month until the balance hits zero.

Don't worry, a zero-based budget doesn't mean you have zero money. It just means you've planned what all your money will do for you throughout the month.

Just remember that this is *your* budget. The intent is for you to have a clear plan for how you will spend *your* money. Done right, a budget isn't restrictive—it actually gives you permission to spend your money. **When you have a plan, spending money is fun instead of frantic.**

download EveryDollar

CHOICES
ARE THE GIFT THAT KEEP ON GIVING—THEY EITHER GIVE A GREAT FUTURE

OR FUTURE CONSEQUENCES.

— JADE WARSHAW

INSURANCE MATTERS

Let's take a few minutes to talk about insurance because having the right kinds of insurance really does matter. This is really important because your insurance costs will have a dramatic impact on your budget. **And the wrong choice when it comes to insurance can become a dumb choice really quickly.**

You need to make room in your budget for insurance. Listen, nobody likes talking about insurance, because we feel like we pay a bunch of money for something we don't really need. It almost feels like we're wasting money.

But you need to think of insurance as paying a company to take on financial risk instead of you having to do it. **You pay a small monthly insurance premium to a company that agrees to pay for a large financial loss if it occurs.** Basically, you're paying for a layer of protection that will take the hit for you if or when something bad, like a car accident, happens.

So, what kinds of insurance do you need right now? While you're in college, there are three basic types of insurance you should absolutely have in place. You may already have these through your parents' insurance policies, but don't assume so. Talk with them about what they cover for you, and then make sure you pick up any that are left.

HEALTH INSURANCE

Health insurance is expensive, but it's necessary. Nobody plans to get sick or have an accident—but it happens. Medical insurance helps pay for your doctor visits, prescriptions, and hospital expenses. If you go to the emergency room without insurance, you'll find out what *expensive* really means! Health insurance helps cover those large medical expenses.

AUTO INSURANCE

If you drive a car, you need auto insurance. Period. There are two kinds: liability and collision. You really need them both. Liability insurance pays to repair or replace someone else's property and covers others' medical costs if you cause an accident. Collision coverage pays to repair or replace your car if you're in an accident that you caused or if you get hit by an uninsured driver.

RENTERS INSURANCE

Renters insurance (or contents insurance) covers your stuff if it's stolen or damaged. If you're living in a dorm at school, your parents' homeowners insurance should cover your stuff. But if you're renting an apartment or house off campus, you definitely need renters insurance. Plus, it only costs $14–30 per month, depending on where you live. That's super cheap considering what it would cost to replace all of your stuff should something happen.

BUDGET-FRIENDLY DATE IDEAS

You don't have to bust your budget—or go into debt—to enjoy a date. **With a little bit of effort, you can find discounts or coupons to help lower the costs of some activities.** After all, if the purpose of your date is to get to know someone and hang out together, then spending a bunch of money to have a good time doesn't make much sense.

To help you out, here's a list of twenty fun date ideas that are either free or won't cost you a lot of money. Try one of these or explore some other options.

1. **Find a nearby town or city to visit and explore.**
2. **Go for a bike ride together.**
3. **Binge-watch your favorite series with a bowl of popcorn and soft drinks.**
4. **Hang some hammocks and enjoy relaxing and talking together.**
5. **Challenge another couple to a dessert bake-off.**
6. **Explore a nearby state or national park.**
7. **Go on a picnic.**
8. **Watch or play intramural sports together.**
9. **Pick an organization that means something to you both and volunteer.**
10. **Look for free local events at parks or museums.**

11. Find discount tickets to a botanical garden or zoo.

12. Learn to dance (swing, ballroom, salsa) with instructional videos on YouTube.

13. Go bowling, play mini golf, or toss a Frisbee.

14. Go for a run in the rain.

15. Go for a hike and take pictures of nature.

16. See a movie at a discount theater.

17. Read and discuss a book together.

18. Visit a local farmers market, fruit orchard, flea market, or community yard sale.

19. Have a game night at a local coffee shop.

20. Tailgate at a college football game.

$98 is the average cost of a **dinner-and-movie date** in the U.S.[36]

05

MONEY ISN'T MOSTLY ABOUT MATH,
IT MOSTLY ABOUT MINDSET.

MISTAKE NO. FIVE
NO MONEY

NO
MONEY

MISTAKE FIVE

MONEY ISN'T MOSTLY ABOUT MATH,
IT MOSTLY ABOUT MINDSET.

FUTURE YOU WILL SAY "THANKS"

I just shared the truth about why having a plan for your money is so important for your present and your future. **All of this might make perfect sense to you.** You're on board with these ideas, and everything is clicking for you. That's fantastic!

But let's be real for a moment. I can imagine that you might be protesting and questioning everything I've told you. I can even hear you heckling, "Carpe diem! Live like there's no tomorrow!" Listen, I understand where you're coming from. I used to say, "YOLO, baby!" I wanted to seize the day too.

There's a part of each of us that just wants to push back against budgets and plans—and anything related to personal finances. We just want to spend our money and enjoy today the way we want. Right?

Are you one of the people pushing back? If so, I understand. I'm like the substitute teacher who assigns you homework instead of letting you off the hook by watching a movie. Trust me when I say there are no hard feelings if you're reluctant, but I do want to make sure we understand each other.

The fact is, these sayings—and others—all have such an amazing ring to them! And in some way, I agree with every single one. But when it comes to these catchphrases, their meaning isn't just in the eye of the beholder. The meaning is all in the maturity of the eye of the beholder. Let me explain.

An immature person hears a phrase like "carpe diem" or "YOLO" and takes it as their permission slip to wild out. This particular grad thinks, *Yes! I'm finally free. It's time to do my thing! I'm only eighteen once, and I'm only in college once, so I may as well enjoy myself. There's no such thing as a dumb choice because I'm simply living in the moment.*

The mindset of doing what you want now so you can enjoy this moment of your life is appealing. **But you need to realize that your life is more than just this moment.** What will future you think about some of the choices you're making in this moment? Good question.

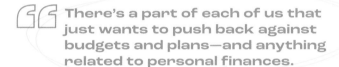

> There's a part of each of us that just wants to push back against budgets and plans—and anything related to personal finances.

Maybe your mindset is a bit more noble. For you, this focus on *now* means there's no risk too big when it comes to education. **This grad isn't interested in goofing off. This grad has goals!** You want to shoot your shot at the university of your dreams not just because your friends will be there but because their engineering department is one of the best in the country.

Sure, you've imagined that your social life could be amazing, but this school could give you the status and edge you think you need to succeed. You can't put a price on that! So you throw caution to the wind and commit to $100K of student loan debt for an undergrad degree, thinking, *Hopefully, I'll end up with a great job and can pay back the student loan fast. Either way, I can figure out the money part later.*

This person isn't thinking about the full impact of this cause-and-effect equation because they're not factoring in risk. Like, $100,000 of risk! **This person is certainly not considering that choices are the gifts that keep on giving.** Your choices either give you a great future or bring future consequences.

The mature person understands that thinking about today is not the same as permission for reckless behavior. The mature grad understands that the money part doesn't wait for later—the money part starts today! The mature grad thinks, *I only live once, and I want to get it right—I want to do my best. I want to get everything out of this college experience that I can to set myself up for success. Living my best life starts with making the best choices, not choices that could set me back or have negative consequences over the long haul.*

Here's some more real talk: **I've not met anyone who said, "Jade, I want to end up hundreds of thousands of dollars in debt, make $40,000 a year, and feel buried under a mountain of payments."** Not one person. Ever.

When you decide to live with a mature mindset, you truly have no regrets. **Trust me, there *is* a way to have fun, get the best education possible, and feel like you're living your best life without carrying a backpack full of debt when you graduate from college.**

I WAS DREADING THE FACT THAT I WAS GOING TO OWE **SO MUCH** MONEY WHEN I GOT OUT OF SCHOOL!

— **AMARI**

FROM *BORROWED FUTURE* DOCUMENTARY

TEN REASONS TO SAVE CASH

Saving money is important. **We all know we should save money, but we come up with lots of reasons why we don't.** And let's face it: Not having money causes lots of stress. In fact, a recent survey indicates that 57% of college students would have trouble covering a $500 emergency, and 48% have a hard time concentrating on their schoolwork because of their financial situation.[37] Talk about stressed!

Here are ten reasons you should start saving money now—while you're in college—so you can avoid that money stress:

1. **Money doesn't grow on trees.**
   In order to have money, you need to work and save some of your earnings (unless you have a magic tree).

2. **Cash in the bank feels good.**
   You get a sense of security (and even experience less stress) when you have cash to handle emergencies.

3. **Saving changes you.**
   Saving money builds character by helping you become more responsible and independent.

4. **You'll want to buy a car.**
   Set savings goals and pay cash for a car! You'll avoid thousands of dollars of interest on a car loan.

5. **You'll want more than cafeteria food.**
   You may want to go out to eat and expand your dining options.

6. College is expensive.

Pay cash for your education instead of using student loans (you may even get a discount!).

7. Weekends require cash.

Driving home for a visit, doing laundry, or heading out with friends means you'll need some money.

8. You'll want to buy stuff.

With cash, you'll be able to buy clothes and technology without going into debt.

9. Road trips don't pay for themselves.

Hitting the road for spring break or an away game means you'll need to buy gas and snacks.

10. Driving a car is expensive.

From putting gas in the tank to paying for repairs and maintenance, cars are not cheap.

The average cost for a check engine light-related repair is

$424 [38]

THE FIVE FOUND- ATIONS

When it comes to handling your money wisely, you need to have some priorities. While you're in college, you can stick to **The Five Foundations—a proven framework for a money plan that will help you win with money!***

1 SAVE A $500 EMERGENCY FUND

Set aside money in a bank savings account to help you cover emergency expenses.

2 GET OUT AND STAY OUT OF DEBT

Cut up any credit cards you might have and stay out of debt for life!

* The Five Foundations are Ramsey Education's basic steps (in *Foundations in Personal Finance*) that any student can and should follow in order to kick-start their money success!

CASH IS KING

DEBT IS NORMAL

BE WEIRD

3 PAY CASH FOR YOUR CAR

Don't take out a car loan or lease a car. Pay cash for a car and own it outright.

4 PAY CASH FOR COLLEGE

Make it your goal to graduate from college without any school debt.

5 BUILD WEALTH AND GIVE

It's important to get in the habit of saving and giving away money early in life.

 Remember: The money habits you develop now will impact your financial security and the way you handle money in the future.

LIFE IS ALWAYS UNPREDICTABLE

Having money in the bank is super important. Why? Because emergencies are going to happen. **The question is not *if* an emergency expense will pop up but *when*.** It's always best to have cash on hand to handle life's emergencies.

The scary reality is that 49% of Americans report having at least $1,000 in savings for emergencies—**but 33% have no savings at all**![39] That's not where you want to find yourself in the event of an emergency. Trust me on that!

Knowing what to do (saving money) is only going to help you if you actually put what you know into practice—and get some money in the bank.

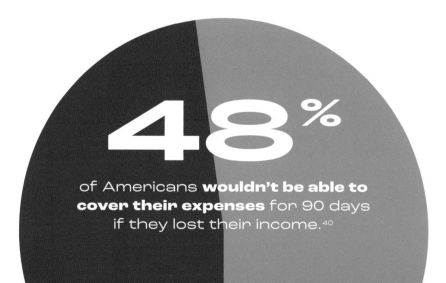

48% of Americans **wouldn't be able to cover their expenses** for 90 days if they lost their income.[40]

PERSONAL FINANCE IS **80**% **BEHAVIOR** AND 20% HEAD KNOWLEDGE.

— DAVE RAMSEY

GIVING IS IMPORTANT

You don't have to spend much time on social media before you see a bunch of selfies and other pictures showing how happy everyone appears to be with their lives . . . and their stuff. **With all the focus on self in the world today, it can be tempting to think that life is all about you.** I hate to burst your bubble, but it's not.

Thinking everything is about you can turn you into a selfish person—and let's face it, selfish people aren't much fun to be around. **Here's a great way to become less selfish: Become more *selfless* by giving to others.**

When it comes to money, there are three basic things you can do with it: **spend it, save it, and give it away.**

A good rule of thumb for giving money is 10% of your income. But giving goes way beyond money. If you don't really have much of an income or you're seriously worried about how to pay for your next meal, then find some other ways to give that don't cost anything. **That could mean giving your time or your talents.**

Think about what you have to offer, even if it's not something tangible. **Giving is one of the most important things you can do, so make it a priority!**

WAYS YOU CAN GIVE TO OTHERS

This isn't an exhaustive list, but here are some ways you can be a little more selfless by giving to others—and these won't cost you any money:

- Volunteer at a homeless shelter.
- Deliver meals to the elderly.
- Visit, sing, or serve at a senior adult care facility.
- Organize an event to raise money for a local charity.
- Volunteer at a food bank or food pantry.
- Wear a fun costume and visit children at a hospital.
- Organize a community cleanup event.
- Volunteer with an after-school program for kids.
- Conduct a shoe or clothing drive for a local charity.
- Volunteer at a local library.
- Coach a youth sports team.
- Volunteer at a local animal shelter.
- Tutor children after school.
- Deliver stuffed animals to a children's hospital.

WE LITERALLY DID NOT HAVE ENOUGH MONEY TO BUY GROCERIES . . . ALL THE CREDIT CARDS WERE **MAXED OUT.** WE HAD NO MONEY.

— JOSIAH

FROM *BORROWED FUTURE* DOCUMENTARY

LIFE IS EXPENSIVE

Fast-forward to your life after college. It's going to be great! You'll be done with school and won't have to worry about cramming for exams anymore. You'll be working and have plenty of time and money to do whatever you want, right?

Hold up—it's time for a reality check. Right now, you probably have big plans for your future—including a big income from your dream job. You can't wait to get started!

It's not uncommon for college students to think they'll make at least $100,000 a year in their first full-time job out of college. That sure would be nice! But that's not reality for most students.

The average first-job salary for a college graduate is just $47,000 per year.[41] That's not bad, but it's also not the reality for lots of college grads. Many job fields pay closer to $37,000–40,000 a year, so it's best not to have your heart set on getting a high-paying job right out of school.

On the next two pages, **let's take a look at how your income will break down with some real-life expenses you'll have when you graduate**. Then take a look at the impact debt can have if you buy into society's definition of "normal." Remember, "normal" includes student loan debt, credit card debt, and a car payment.

AVERAGE GRADUATE BUDGET

INCOME

Monthly Income (after taxes) .... $ 3,166
Based on an average annual salary of $47,000

EXPENSES

Giving	$	320
Groceries	$	300
Utilities (shared with a roommate)	$	150
Housing (shared with a roommate)	$	750
Gas/Transportation	$	275
Car Insurance	$	300
Renters Insurance	$	20
Car Maintenance	$	150
Cell Phone	$	80
Doctor Visits	$	140
Fun Money	$	75
Clothing	$	50
Entertainment	$	40
Restaurants	$	50
Miscellaneous/Unexpected Expenses	$	100
Savings	$	200

TOTAL

Income	$	3,166
Expenses (without debt)	- $	3,000

MONEY IN THE BANK

$166

Note: For a zero-based budget, that means you still have money that needs an assignment.

DEBT IS THE DIFFERENCE BETWEEN FINANCIAL PEACE AND PAYMENTS.

DEBT PAYMENTS

Student Loans	$ 412
Car Loan	$ 520
Credit Cards	$ 159

TOTAL

Income	$ 3,166
Expenses (including debt)	- $ 4,091

-$925

THIS IS BAD

CREATE YOUR OWN MONEY MANTRA

When you break it down, all of those cliché mantras I mentioned earlier are about living in the moment. **The idea is that all those moments strung together create your life experience. In this case, it's your college life experience.** And you want that to be the best it can be—not just while you're in school but for the years and decades afterward.

Years from now, you'll want to look back and think, *Man, that was freakin' awesome.* You don't want to be the one thinking, *Man, I was such a screw-up in college,* or *I partied way too hard,* or *I went into so much debt.* **Your goal should be to graduate from college with no regrets—and no consequences following you into your post-college years** (like never-ending student loan debt payments).

So, maybe it's time to come up with your own mantra for your college experience. One that truly embodies what it should be, all things considered. **It should be fun, full of learning, free from debt, filled with growth, but still totally engaged in the moment.** If I had to take a swing at it, I'd say something like: **I'm living my best life now so I can live my best life later.**

You want to have fun, and you want to enjoy your college experience—but not at the expense of your future life. **Take it from someone who knows, your future self doesn't want to pay the piper for your current college self.**

You don't have to wait until you're older to figure out the money part and live your best life. Living your best life means figuring it out now. **Listen, this money stuff isn't that complicated. You can do it.** It won't be perfect, but it will be intentional, and it will keep you on track.

And if you work to avoid the five mistakes described in this book, you'll be proud of your college experience. **You'll be able to come out of it all and say, "I'm not only a college grad who survived—I'm one who thrived, and I'm living my best life without debt!"**

I'm genuinely excited for you! And in case no one else has said it, **I'm so very proud of you**. The fact that you've taken in all of this information ahead of time is a true game changer. **If you actually put this into practice, watch out world. You're about to be unstoppable!**

Thanks for letting me hang with you during such an exciting time in your life. And thanks for letting me share my heart with you. **Now, put these things into practice and avoid these five mistake in college.** Good luck out there! I'm rooting for you!

🖥 jadewarshaw.com
📷 ✕ jadewarshaw
f jadewarshawpersonality
♪ @jadewarshaw

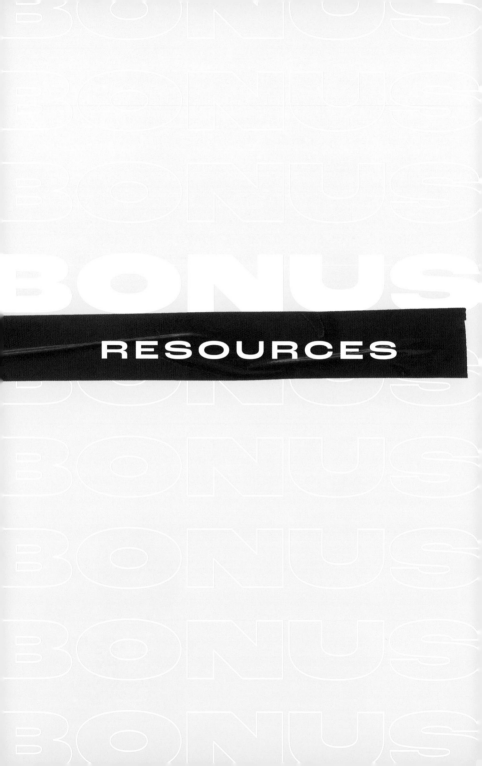

BONUS

RESOURCES

STUDENT LOAN DEBT IN AMERICA TOPS

1,700,000,000,000

Do you even know how to read that number? **That's $1.7 trillion.** And that's how much student loan debt Americans are drowning in.

But not you. A new generation is waking up to the dark side of the student loan industry that's been out to get us from day one.

Watch Ramsey's eye-opening documentary, *Borrowed Future.*

Discover how to buck the system, beat the stats, and **take back control of your future**—for good.

BUDGETING FOR COLLEGE LIFE AND BEYOND

Whether you're a new college student or getting your first grown-up paycheck, you can be in control of your money—no matter what pops up—with **EveryDollar**.

Grocery runs? No problem.
Bedroom makeover? Covered.
Unexpected Uber ride? Tip included.

The EveryDollar budget app helps you plan for it all. And it's what I use to stay on top of my finances too.

And guess what? **It's totally free to start.**
Download it today in the App Store or Google Play.

download

NOTES

MISTAKE 01 // STUDENT LOAN DEBT

1. "Consumer Credit Outstanding (Levels)," Federal Reserve, accessed May 13, 2024, https://www.federalreserve.gov/releases/g19/hist/cc_hist_memo_levels.html.

2. Chris Horymski, "Americans Shed More Than 10% of Total Student Loan Debt Since March 2020," Experian, last modified August 25, 2023, https://www.experian.com/blogs/ask-experian/state-of-student-loan-debt/.

3. "Trends in College Pricing and Student Aid 2023," College Board, November 2023, https://research.collegeboard.org/media/pdf/Trends%20Report%202023%20Updated.pdf.

4. "Federal Student Loan Portfolio Summary," Federal Student Loan Portfolio, Federal Student Aid, accessed March 7, 2024, https://studentaid.gov/data-center/student/portfolio.

5. Melanie Hanson, "College Dropout Rates," Education Data Initiative, last modified October 29, 2023, https://educationdata.org/college-dropout-rates.

6. "Interest Rates for Direct Loans First Disbursed Between July 1, 2024 and June 30, 2025," Federal Student Aid, last modified May 14, 2024, https://fsapartners.ed.gov/knowledge-center/library/electronic-announcements/2024-05-14/interest-rates-direct-loans-first-disbursed-between-july-1-2024-and-june-30-2025.

7. Federal Student Aid, "Interest Rates for Direct Loans."

8. "College Student Employment," National Center for Education Statistics, last modified May 2022, https://nces.ed.gov/programs/coe/indicator/ssa.

9. Sandra Craft, "College Dropout Rates," Think Impact, last modified October 4, 2021, https://www.thinkimpact.com/college-dropout-rates/.

MISTAKE 02 // CREDIT CARDS

10. "Zero Liability," Visa, accessed May 30, 2024, https://usa.visa.com/pay-with-visa/visa-chip-technology-consumers/zero-liability-policy.html.

11. "Zero Liability Protection," Mastercard, accessed May 30, 2024, https://www.mastercard.us/en-us/personal/get-support/zero-liability-terms-conditions.html.

12. "What's in My FICO® Scores?" MyFICO, accessed May 21, 2024, https://www.myfico.com/credit-education/whats-in-your-credit-score.

13. "Quarterly Report on Household Debt and Credit: 2023: Q4," New York Fed, February 2024, https://www.newyorkfed.org/medialibrary/interactives/householdcredit/data/pdf/HHDC_2023Q4.

14. "Bankcard Balances Surge Past $1 Trillion as All Risk Tiers Drive Up Their Credit Card Balances," TransUnion, last modified February 15, 2024, https://www.transunion.com/blog/q4-2023-credit-industry-insights-report.

15. "Economic Well-Being of U.S. Households in 2022," Board of Govenors of the Federal Reserve System, May 2023, https://www.federalreserve.gov/publications/files/2022-report-economic-well-being-us-households-202305.pdf.

16. "Terms of Credit at Commercial Banks and Finance Companies," Federal Reserve, last modified May 7, 2024, https://www.federalreserve.gov/releases/g19/hist/cc_hist_tc_levels.html.

17. Rick Popely, "Car Depreciation: How Much Value Does a Car Lose Per Year?" last modified February 3, 2021, https://www.carfax.com/blog/car-depreciation.

18. "Why Market to College Students?" DormAdvertising, accessed May 13, 2024, https://www.dormadvertising.com/blog/why-market-to-college-students.

MISTAKE 03 // DUMB CHOICES

19. "How Prepared Are High School Graduates for Their Next Step?" YouScience, accessed May 13, 2024, https://resources.youscience.com/rs/806-BFU-539/images/2022_PostGradReadiness_Report_Pt1.pdf.

20. College Board, "Trends in College Pricing and Student Aid 2023."

21. Imed Bouchrika, PhD, "What Is Included in Room and Board in College: How to Cover the Costs in 2024?" last modified April 17, 2024, https://research.com/education/what-is-included-in-room-and-board-in-college#3.

22. College Board, "Trends in College Pricing and Student Aid 2023."

23. Bouchrika, "What Is Included in Room and Board in College?"

24. College Board, "Trends in College Pricing and Student Aid 2023."

25. "Survey: The Ever-Growing Power of Reviews (2023 Edition)," Power Reviews, accessed May 21, 2024, https://www.powerreviews.com/power-of-reviews-2023/.

26. "Impulse Spending Report: Americans Are Shopping Smarter in 2023," Slickdeals, last modified July 26, 2023, https://money.slickdeals.net/surveys/slickdeals-impulse-spending-survey-2023/.

27. "Captives Recapture Total Vehicle Financing Market Share in the U.S.," August 31, 2023, https://www.experianplc.com/newsroom/press-releases/2023/captives-recapture-total-vehicle-financing-market-share-in-the-us.

MISTAKE 04 // NO PLAN

28. "The State of Personal Finance in America Q2 2023," Ramsey Solutions, last modified November 16, 2023, https://www.ramseysolutions.com/budgeting/state-of-personal-finance.

29. "Labor Force Participation Rates of College Students Differ by Enrollment Status and Type of College," U.S. Bureau of Labor Statistics, last modified May 24, 2023, https://www.bls.gov/opub/ted/2023/labor-force-participation-rates-of-college-students-differ-by-enrollment-status-and-type-of-college.htm.

30. "Delivery Driver Salary in United States," Indeed, accessed May 16, 2024, https://www.indeed.com/career/delivery-driver/salaries.

31. "Barista Salary in United States," Indeed, accessed May 16, 2024, https://www.indeed.com/career/barista/salaries.

32. "Dog Walker Salary in United States," Indeed, accessed May 16, 2024, https://www.indeed.com/career/dog-walker/salaries.

33. "Errand Runner Salary," ZipRecruiter, accessed May 16, 2024, https://www.ziprecruiter.com/Salaries/Errand-Runner-Salary.

34. "Tutor Salary in United States," Indeed, accessed May 16, 2024, https://www.indeed.com/career/tutor/salaries.

35. "Retail Sales Associate Salary in United States," Indeed, accessed May 16 ,2024, https://www.indeed.com/career/retail-sales-associate /salaries.

36. Sophie Watson, "Data Study: The Cost of a Date Night in Your State," last modified December 8, 2022, https://www.zoosk.com/date-mix /dating-data/date-night-cost-2021/.

MISTAKE 05 // NO MONEY

37. Carla Fletcher, Allyson Cornett, Jeff Webster, and Bryan Ashton, "Student Financial Wellness Survey: Fall 2022 Semester Results," May 2023, https://www.trelliscompany.org/wp-content/uploads/2023/05 /SFWS-Aggregate-Report_FALL-2022.pdf.

38. "Vehicle Health Index 2024," CarMD, April 24, 2024, https://www.carmd. com/assets/pdf/VHI/2024/CarMD_Index_APR24_042424.pdf.

39. Ramsey Solutions, "State of Personal Finance."

40. Ramsey Solutions, "State of Personal Finance."

41. "Graduate Salary," ZipRecruiter, May 23, 2024, https://www. ziprecruiter.com/Salaries/Graduate-Salary.